LET IT GO

How to let go built-UP NEGATIVE ENERGY and past relationships trauma

By

Elizabeth show

Table of contents

Why letting go is such a tough thing to learn or do?

We love hard so we fall hard. We give all our love to someone who we thought was meant for us. But it seems everything just doesn't happen as we wish. Since the day you bid farewell to each other, You might have been thinking about everything regarding him/her: the place where you first met, the movie which you watched thousand times together, the way you relate with each other, or how he/she said he/she loved you.

But everything is gone.

Our relationships are a huge part of our lives and our well-being and letting go of a significant one can be heartbreaking, to say the least. But when we're caught up in dynamics that don't serve us, we're only limiting ourselves—and letting go is simply the best course of action.

This book will show you the theoretical part of why and how you should let go. And why you should work in sync with emotions and not against it.

I sincerely hope this book give you the ability to learn how to finally let go of your built up sad emotions gradually and you experience the feeling of positivity and detachment from negative energy.

Elizabeth Show

Chapter 1: Surrounded by signs but still denying reality

Denial is like a cloud that obscures the sky. It blocks the truth. It reduces clarity. ~ Gloria Excelsior

When I was a child, my mother always says you can always let go, because whatever was meant for you would surely find its way back to you. But is it always that easy to let go?

My first heartbreak happened in college when my boyfriend whom I trusted with my whole heart decided to sleep with one of my closest friends in our apartment. I'd gone home for thanksgiving the previous week but I decided to return early and make it a surprise because my supposed boyfriend's birthday was the subsequent week. I was so excited cos I knew he would be so happy and surprised to see me. Getting home and meeting the love of my life and my friend unclad laying next to each other was the biggest shock of my life.
Even after getting my heart broken, I still had this tiny or tiniest hope that we could still work out. I started denying the reality of things.

What's denial?
Denial is typically related with rejecting or denying reality or thinking or believing that things "aren't so". During this period our heart takes over our belief system as we make endeavors into adjusting to the idea of life without the person we're losing.

Even though the relationship is over, we don't believe it most of the time.

See, logically, denial may be a kind of unconscious process. You're trying to protect yourself from the things that make you feel out of control by refusing to accept the reality of what's happening in your life.

When living in denial, you may feel protected at that moment but it's only a false and temporary sense of security, it won't make the situation change or disappear. The sole solution is to take control of the situation.

Signs you're in denial:

- Shifting blames on other people for your problem
- Ignoring the pieces of advice and concerns of your loved ones
- Feeling frustrated, annoyed, stressed
- Getting defensive or isolated from people
- Avoiding talking about the situation

How to let go of denial:

- Speaking to someone: The next thing you need to do, once you've fully processed it in your mind is to verbalize it. Talk to someone about it. Get it off your chest, out of your head. Someone can hold you "accountable" in a way then. This part is very important. When you verbalize it, you share it with someone else, you make it real. You're no longer hiding away. You have to recognize it, acknowledge it, and act there on. Otherwise it's too easy to travel back into your head and push it away, which is precisely what denial wants us to do and drives us to do. Just know that denial doesn't always have to have a bad outcome when you face it. It isn't always something to fear. You frequently fear confronting it because it creates change and it pushes you out of your safety net which is pretty scary. And you might ask, but hold up a second, what's confronting about letting go of the denial you had around what your past relationship was really like? Surely that's a good thing if you can see that and express that. It's changing the way you saw the relationship and what it all meant. And removing those tinted glasses isn't always nice to see, it can make you feel like you wasted time, or the things you used to believe, weren't true.

- Understanding what you're afraid of: if you want to let go of denial, you must understand why you've been in denial initially . What are you scared of? What are the implications you've been trying to avoid? and what is it about these things that scare you the most.

Once you face up to denial and act on it – you free yourself. But you also can't beat yourself up about it or think, "See, this is why I should have left things..." You

can't leave things. Leaving things is simply passing time,
It doesn't make the issue go away.

Chapter 2: Clouded mind

Holding on to anger is like grasping a hot coal with the intent of
throwing it at someone else; you are the one who gets burned
~ Buddha

After I got my heart broken, for the next few weeks, was consumed with anger. I would say things like I hate him, he'll regret leaving me, I want revenge, they deserve to pay, etc. *"I couldn't bring myself to the fact he cheated cos I thought I found the one, he was the perfect example of the one"*.

Where denial may be seen as a coping mechanism, anger is a masking effect. Anger masks many of the emotions and pain you feel. Your anger may be directed at other people such as your ex or even your loved ones. You may even direct your anger toward inanimate objects. While your rational brain knows the object of your anger isn't at fault, your feelings at that moment are too intense to act accordingly.

Anger may mask itself in feelings like bitterness, resentment, loss of control, pessimism, and irritability. It may not be clear-cut fury or rage.

Not everyone will experience this stage of letting go and others may linger here. As the anger subsides, however, you may begin to think more rationally about what's happening and feel the emotions you've been pushing aside.

It seems like you will never be able to find true happiness again as you don't know how it feels anymore. It's okay to vent out your feelings to yourself and realize what you went through, through your anger and sadness. It's you coming to terms with the breakup. While being furious with whatever happened, may inspire you to want to slam them on social media, lashing out publicly probably isn't going to help you feel better in the long run. Instead, it's likely to leave you with feelings of shame and remorse once you've moved past your fiery feelings.

Here are some ways to channel your anger :

• Do not suppress your feelings: "You might have to find a reason to be mad at the person until you're ready to deal with the feelings of vulnerability and rawness that come with rejection", Maybe you replay the relationship in your mind to uncover all the red flags you ignored in the past, or decide that your ex was a commitment-phobe. What's important is that you've formulated a story for yourself to make sense of the breakup, even if it's not necessarily the complete picture.

- Productively move through your anger. Sharing your feelings with someone in your support system. Repeating a calming phrase can make it easier to express difficult emotions, including anger and frustration. Try slowly repeating, "Take it easy," or "Everything's going to be okay," the next time you're feeling overwhelmed by a situation. You can do this out loud if you want, but you can also say it under your breath or in your head. You can also keep a list of phrases on your phone for a quick reminder before a stressful work presentation or challenging meeting.

- Discovering new ways to express your feelings: If you are having trouble verbalizing your feelings because most people don't know how to express their feelings verbally. you can try expressing yourself through art, journaling, poetry, listening to music, and dancing.
- Seek help: It's normal and healthy to feel upset and angry from time to time. But if you can't shake a bad mood or constantly feel overwhelmed by anger, it might be time to ask for help. Seeking advice from a therapist if you're able, might be your best bet for moving through your feelings and finding peace.

Chapter 3: "What if"

Bargaining is a defense against the feelings of helplessness experienced after a loss, it happens when people struggle accept the reality of the loss and limits of their control over it ~Sabrina Romanoff, PYSD

After channeling my anger towards working out and writing my journals. Trust me it wasn't easy, at this point I was already relapsing. I started the "what ifs", what if I'd stayed back and not gone home, what if I overreacted, what if I forgive him for hurting you? Things could still work out.

This is the stage where you clutch an irrational hope even when the facts say otherwise. This may be influenced by your inner dialogue or prayer. In simple words, it is what we call the 'what ifs'. With the given example, this is can be once you start saying these words to yourself: 'What if I have forgiven him?', 'What if I'd not gone home and didn't see it?', 'What if I gave it another chance?' This is often the stage where you make those pledges similar as living a decent life, helping the poor, wishing for miracles etc. as an endeavor to bring you back to where you were before. At this stage of letting go, you begin having a glimpse of hope and you can easily trip up and call him but the foremost important thing is to realize that nothing will change if the two of you get back together. Things might look fine at the start but eventually, everything will go back to the way it was.

You will start to fight again, avoid one another, or he will cheat again.

People who enter this stage quickly learn that bargaining doesn't work and inevitably pass on to the next stage.

Here are some ways to get by the bargaining stage:

- Give yourself time: With time, your pain will probably come more manageable, and the idea of accepting circumstances outside of your control may be more tolerable.

- Avoid ruminating over these thoughts A good way to cope during this stage is to try to get perspective and emotional distance from these thoughts, rather of perseverating over them. You can share these thoughts with a friend or someone you're close with to help you in weighing them.

- You can also seek help from a therapist and they're also some helpful support group that may share similar grief which may be helpful.

Chapter 4: A Glimpse Of Reality

No storm, not even the one in your life can last forever, the storm is just passing over
~ Iyanla Vanzant

The end of a relationship can flip your world upside down and trigger a range of emotions. At this stage, you come to the terms with the fact that the situation is not going to change. It's a time for reflection, you might want to coil up into your shell. However, you may find yourself feeling sad and low, If you're grieving the loss of a relationship or someone you cared about, everything may feel bleak and hopeless and you may not feel like doing things you formerly cared about. You may feel overwhelmed and find it tough to get out of bed and go about your daily activities. However, it won't change until you realize the reality of things.

Recognizing signs of depression after a breakup and getting help for it can decrease the risk of complications. If left unattended, you may rely on alcohol or drugs and unhealthy activities to numb emotional pain. Depression can also affect your physical health. You may experience pain in some parts of your body system. Recurrent stress can weaken your immune system and make you more exposed to infections and illnesses. Stress eating can cause excessive weight gain and increase your risk for diabetes.

Signs of depression:

- Feeling overwhelmed
- Impassiveness
- Withdrawing from other people
- Closing off from the world
- Loss of appetite
- Low self-esteem
- Insomnia
- Suicidal thoughts

Coping with depression

- Stay involved: Push yourself to stay involved with your friends and the people that care about you, social connections can help your depression level from deteriorating. Go for walk, watch movies or even a karaoke night can lift up your mood.

- Don't avoid your feelings: Work on accepting all the feelings that come up. No feeling is right or wrong. Trying to suppress your feelings would do you no good and it might make the depression worse.

- Keep yourself busy: Physical activities can boost your energy level and immune system. Exercising can increase the production of endorphins in your body which can improve your mood. You can also explore hobbies and keep your mind occupied. If you're feeling depressed, read a book, go for a walk, or start a project around the house.

- Seek help: If the feeling gets overwhelming and leaves no space for anything differently, it may be helpful to seek professional support because there are effective treatments available. You should consider seeking help if you tend to forget monuments of the loss, continue to have trouble accepting the loss even after six months, feel numb, empty, overwhelmed by rage, or have thoughts of self-murder.

Chapter 5: The light at the end of tunnel

to love life, to love it even
when you have no stomach for it
and everything you've held dear

Whew! At last, You did it. You've conquered and are wholeheartedly ready to move on with your life. Of course, it doesn't mean there won't be tough moments, days, or weeks ahead as you adapt to life post-breakup. It's impeccably normal to want to date again, indeed if it's accompanied by some mixed feelings.

Following up on your work from the former stages will make things better. " By journaling, exercising, seeking professional help, the break-up pain will slowly but surely dissipates. Getting to this stage is a sign that you're beginning to come to terms with the situation.

Eventually, you'll be able to accept the reality; the two of you broke up and he or she wasn't the one for you. You need to realize that when you find the one, this chase and struggle will be over and you'll eventually realize why all those before demanded to be left in history. Take out time to fall in love with yourself; indulge in self-care, try out a new hobby, take a trip, and get a new hairstyle.

You need to understand that you'll crave the closeness and familiarity of your ex for some time. The first few weeks or even months are common triggers. Also, anything or things you typically do together will remind you of your significant other. Those feelings of craving have nothing to do with the person, but rather with the human condition(the way we feel normally). You've created a gap in your day-to-day life and that will feel uncomfortable for a while until you induce a new routine and fill that gap. I recommend filling that gap with healthy actions that support your alignment. After a time, you can reflect on lessons learned from this relationship, as you move on to a healthier match in the future.

Chapter 6: Moving on

The choice isn't to move on—life moves whether I want it to or not. No, the choice is to look forward, not backward, to take a step because refusing to move won't draw the past nearer, only postpone better days."
~Caroline George

The problem is that most of us have been taught to pretend we're okay even when we aren't so we don't allow ourselves to process the feelings that go with this loss. And that impacts our capability to have healthy connections moving forward because we start to carry " unhealthy baggage ".
We may act like we don't mind and say we don't care, but we normally do. Or we try things to help with the pain – courting someone in a different way, drinking, eating or barely eating, watching sad films or listening to sad songs, shopping, working out exorbitantly, making ourselves over sleeping.
These behaviors may temporarily make us feel better, but they don't allow us to get complete with the end of the relationship. Why should we get complete with past connections? So that we can be completely present for current ones. We can take the hurt from a former relationship and bring it into the coming one if we don't completely let go.

Our internal dialogue, the things we say inside of our head, can profoundly affect our mindset and feelings. this is often especially true when going through a hard time, like a tough split-up. attempt to speak kindly to yourself and think positively about the future rather than spending your time lamenting the loss of the relationship or thinking about history. you'll try saying words of affirmation to yourself every day eg "I am healing and strengthening every day", "Happiness is a choice, and today I choose to be happy".

This may feel silly because everyone wants to be happy, right? But this is not always the case when getting over a split-up. you'll find yourself wallowing in feelings of sadness or rage about your breakup and taking comfort in them. But, sooner or later, it'll only hurt you. By saying the expression "I want to be happy, " you remind yourself that making an effort towards feeling good pays off, indeed if being sad over your relationship brings you some short-term pleasure.

Within the early stages of getting over a breakup, you'll spend plenty of time figuring out why your relationship ended. Often, in the early aftermath of a breakup, your beliefs about the relationship are not quite accurate. While moving on, you'd like to be brutally honest with yourself about the relationship's flaws that caused it to end. Most of the time, relationships end for an honest reason.

And, if you cannot think of any reasons why it ended and you feel that your partner broke up with you out of the blue, it shows that there was a flaw because your partner didn't feel the same way about the relationship.

Trying to wrap it around your head and see the relationship for what it was can be very difficult.

After a breakup, you'll feel very compelled to spend all of your time thinking about the past and your former relationship. But, therein lies the problem- your relationship along with your ex is in the past, and no matter how much time you spend thinking about it or being upset over it, you cannot change the fact that you and your former partner are now broken up.

It is not easy but do your best to stay focus on moving ahead, don't get stuck in the past . it's hard to believe the wake of a breakup, but you will get over it eventually. And, your next relationship are going to be even better because of the lessons you learned from your past relationship.

If you've a hard time managing your emotions independently, don't hesitate to reach out to a therapist or counselor. Everyone has the strength within them to get over a breakup, but a therapist can facilitate your find it within yourself. Breakups are always hard, but you'll take comfort in knowing that you simply can, and will, get over it in time.

You deserve to wake up with a smile on your face.
You deserve to feel you're excited to be alive
You deserve to be excited about your life, your dreams and your goals.
You deserve to be loved, you deserve to find the person who makes an effort with you and chooses you all the time.
You deserve to attract things you desire.
You're not a magnet for pain, failure or hardships.
You're not meant to live a sad life forever.
You're not meant to live your life based on anyone's opinion
You deserve to believe in yourself enough to know you're different.
You deserve to know your worth and your value and walk away from people who can't see it.
You've to believe you've qualities that set you apart from everyone, never compare yourself to anyone.
Don't believe people who tell you that no one is happy or that happiness is an illusion
YOU DESERVE MORE!!!

Epilogue

Now is the time for you to grow and be independent:
to unzip your dress, to try and do all the housework
on your own, to understand more about yourself, and
to pursue your dreams.

Moving on and letting go is never easy but with time
and determination you can be in control of your
situation. Don't dwell in your past and don't allow
them influence your decisions.

That acceptance is letting go. It's understanding that you're better off without this person having immediate access to you. And from this place of acceptance, you're able to free up the attention and energy you were giving this person and put it toward things that bring you peace and joy.

Sometimes you need to take responsibility for your own happiness, it takes a long time for you to realize how truly miserable you are and even longer to see that it doesn't have to be that way, you've to give up everything(built up bad energy)only then can you begin to find a way to be happy.

Let yourself, love, in peace, you shouldn't try to reduce how you express your emotions because of fear of being taken for granted. So please don't stress your mind, if whatever relationship or situation-ship you're in doesn't work for you, **Walk Away.**

No one is worth losing yourself. Be present and enjoy every moment in your life.